ALEX
and the
DINOSAUR
PRINTS

ALEX MIKA

First paperback edition January 2021

Cover and book design by Asya Blue

ISBN 978-1-953017-00-0 (paperback)
ISBN 978-1-953017-01-7 (e-book)
ISBN 978-1-953017-02-4 (audio book)

ISBN 979-8-593753-21-2 (Amazon paperback)

www.alexmika.com

TO PLUTO: YOU WILL ALWAYS
BE A PLANET TO ME.

lex and the Dinosaur Prints would be a decent band name, wouldn't it? We could write a song called "Rock Star" about the asteroid that killed the dinosaurs (sung, of course, from the perspective of the asteroid). Some other songs would be "The Pterodactyl Shuffle," "Benny and the Rex," and we would always warm up with dinosaur scales. Our influence on modern culture would be unparalleled, and we would instantly be admitted into the pantheon of pop idols, residing beside The Eagles, The Beatles, Flock of Seagulls, and the rest of The Animals.

Small carnivores were probably the smartest dinosaurs. That's scientific speculation, not anti-vegetarian propaganda.

The Flintstone's car ran on running feet. It probably didn't run on fossil fuels because they didn't want to upset their pet, Dino.

I've stayed up many nights wondering what sounds the dinosaurs emitted. Films like *Jurassic Park* feature roars and rumbles, screams and screeches, but what if the mighty Brachiosaurus peeped? Did the velociraptors howl at the moon in packs as they rustled through the swaying ferns, searching for prey? Did the perched pterodactyl sing like a thrush in the trees before its massive body broke the branches? What if the T-Rex nervously cooed and clucked as it rested on its eggs, thumping its tail on the ground as it waited to hear a "crack?"

Of all the creatures roaming Earth today, I would have never guessed that birds are the dinosaurs' closest relatives. I always assumed that lizards and iguanas carried the family torch, but on a recent visit to a farm, it finally made sense to me. Look into the eyes of a chicken and tell me you don't see the shadow of a velociraptor.

Feathers evolved from scales like those found on alligators. Although dinosaur feathers were not as complex and branched as modern bird feathers, these proto feathers developed from evolutionary pressures to preserve body heat. As the feathers became more intricate and asymmetrical, they began to aid in the flight of winged dinosaurs, from which birds eventually evolved.

Why do so many people reject the hypothesis that the T-Rex may have had feathers? Truth be told, I don't actually know how many people refute this, or if this is even a hot-button issue amongst amateur dinosaur enthusiasts, but I think it is safe to assume that a feathered king of the dinosaurs is not what the huddled masses imagine. They picture the massive, leathery beast portrayed in films, images and cartoons, and any mention of feathers immediately results in cognitive dissonance. It's like the T-Rex is this sort of prehistoric Rambo. If Rambo could have his pecs out while wasting away his enemies, it makes sense to assume that the T-Rex was similarly bare-chested in its hunt. But why does adding feathers suddenly make the creature less intimidating? Why are feathers considered a sign of weakness? Have these people never had an angry emu chase after them?

THE GREAT EMU WAR, PART ONE: (2 November – 10 December 1932) was an unsuccessful attempt by the Australian government to curb the population of emus, which were wreaking havoc on the agricultural community. During the Great Depression, farmers were subsidized to grow wheat to prevent a collapse of the industry. When wheat prices dropped, tension between the farmers and the government ensued. The situation was further exacerbated by the advent of the emu post-mating season migration; the birds consumed crops and left gaps in fences to allow for rabbits to continue the destruction. In desperation, the farmers pleaded with the government to act. In October of 1932, Major G. P. W. Meredith of the Seventh Heavy Battery of the Royal Australian Artillery was placed in command

of a military operation. With two Lewis guns and ten thousand rounds of ammunition, the troops advanced on the feathery friends. It began to rain, however, and the birds scattered, creating suboptimal conditions for ~~slaughter~~ combat. The ~~massacre~~ battle was postponed.

Some dinosaurs' tails were over 45 feet long. If tails exist for the purpose of maintaining balance, and animals like cats use their tails to fall feet-first, if a dinosaur fell from a tree or a dining room table, would it land on its feet?

THE GREAT EMU WAR, PART TWO: On the Second of November, the rain cleared, and fifty emus were spotted just out of range for the guns. The farmers attempted to herd them in closer so that they would be within firing distance, but the birds scattered and proved difficult targets. Only about a dozen birds were killed that day.

All dinosaurs laid eggs.

FOSSILS: The term "fossil" applies to all signs of past life. It refers to body fossils (bones), soft tissue fossils (skin and organs), imprints (leaf impressions) and ichnofossils (droppings and footprints).

I'm a technological fossil, which is really concerning since I'm expected to be a computer whisperer and digital prodigy like my peers. I don't know how Facebook or Twitter works, and I get upset whenever I have to update my phone because I just got used to the old way. I will say, though, thank heavens for the word processor, because I would hate to deal with getting my fingers black and greasy from adjusting a typewriter's ink ribbon.

I'm technically part of the iPhone generation, but I still remember how to run a VCR, and I preferred the sound of old vinyl records over CD's before the "hipsters" rediscovered them at Urban Outfitters.

Vinyl is a synthetic plastic made in part from crude oil (a fossil fuel).

JAZZ.

Miles, Dizzy and John

may have life everlasting.

They will survive long after

I am gone (if my basement doesn't flood). They rest

on a disc, and spin in euphoria, kicking up

ashes as warm, rubbery mildew

perfume embraces the room.

Their harmonies, so intricate

and exposed like roses in snowless winter,

live and die on the tip of a needle.

When I was a fourth grader, I went through a calligraphy phase. It was my dream to write my masterpieces on parchment, roll it up with stained fingers, stamp it closed with candle wax and bury it for unsuspecting gardeners or archeologists to find (long after my bones turned to dust). My family, as they often do, humored me and bought a small calligraphy starter kit. In this cardboard box was a brown feathered quill, a black ink bottle, four brass tips, a matching brass stamp in the shape of the sun and a red candle. All I needed was some parchment.

We drove to the local office supply store, and asked the sales associate if they had any parchment paper, to which the clock-watching teenager distractedly replied, "Like, uh, for cooking?" No, for writing. He sighed and pointed to the paper aisle. There, we found a stack of tacky, inflated clipart images of a scroll printed onto one side of what was probably just white office paper. This was not worthy of even my first-grade amateurish manuscripts, let alone the polished work of a fourth grader. We purchased the paper reluctantly (to practice, I consoled myself), and I decided I would figure out a way to make my own.

At this point in my life, my experience with computers was limited to school-wide standardized exams and coolmathgames.com, but I managed to find an article on how to make parchment paper in an oven. I placed the paper on baking sheets, turned up the oven (thankfully, not to 451 degrees), and watched them turn a crispy amber.

HOME-MADE PARCHMENT PAPER RECIPE

Just like grandma never made.

The Ingredients:
- Piece(s) of paper
- ¼ cup hot tea or coffee
- A large baking sheet
- A towel you won't feel bad about staining
- An oven

The Process:

1. Preheat your oven, setting it at the lowest possible temperature.
2. Place the paper(s) on the baking sheet.
3. Pour the tea or coffee on the sheet, making sure it soaks the paper evenly.
4. Let it sit for a few minutes.
5. Remove all excess liquid with the towel; there should be no puddles on the sheet.

6. Place the sheet in the oven and let it bake until the paper is dry, and the edges start to curl.

7. Take the sheet out, turn off your oven, and enjoy! Best served at room temperature.

I started keeping a kind of journal recently. I call it my "mouse nest." On these legal pads, one would find the mental equivalents of plastic bag bits, seed cases and chewed-up aglets. These are thoughts, half-thoughts, single firings of a neuron, snippets of conversations, musings, eavesdroppings, ideas, lines of verse, lines of prose, lines crossed out and pen marks smudged. More accurately, this journal is more of a bog than a nest. I collect these fragments, and most of them decay before settling amongst the sludge. Some lucky bits of peat reach that sacred place. The pressure of nearing deadlines turns these fragments into lignite, and I begin to sift through the yellow pages, hoping to find within this deposit pieces of coal. Once found, they are processed and heaved into the fire, one by one.

How clean was the air in the Mesozoic Era? The massive ferns must have made the air heavy with a chlorophyllic sweetness.

THE GREAT EMU WAR, PART THREE: The birds began to adapt to their hostile environment. The army observers noticed that the birds were beginning to develop their own formations, with scouts and leaders warning and guiding the emu herds away from the advancing forces. Mounting the guns onto moving trucks to pursue the enemy failed, as the cars could not keep up with the emus. On November 8th, faced with growing discontent from the media and public, as well as unimpressive results, the government decided to end military involvement in the operation.

No one knows the lifespan of a dinosaur. Some scientists speculate they could live for as long as two hundred years.

BODY FOSSILS: Body fossils typically consist of bones or other hard parts of the organism, as tissues are often destroyed by decomposition. Animals with hard shells are more likely to be fossilized; the natural processes often destroy remains before they are sufficiently buried so that they can begin the fossilization process. Once they are buried, the minerals in the bone or shell undergo chemical changes, known as replacement. It is these replacement minerals that are later found by paleontologists (and high school students interested in gardening).

Scientists estimate dinosaur speeds by measuring the distance between footprints. One lethargic individual could screw up the image for the rest of its species.

I would probably be the human equivalent of that dinosaur. If my room and I were the only pieces of evidence proving the existence of humans, future paleontologist notes would probably look something like this:

June 17, 9071

Our digging team has uncovered what appears to be the remains of a yet undocumented species similar to Homo sapiens, along with its burrow (it seems these creatures were burrowers). I will name this species Homo cuniculum. The findings are as follows:

1. Primitive garments - it appears this species did not yet develop fashion sense.

2. A vessel of "Intense Sport Deodorant." This vessel's purpose is not yet clear since there is no evidence supporting the possibility that this creature was active. Further research is required.

3. Four (4) light sources. The species was most likely nocturnal, but not sufficiently adapted to exist in darkness without aid.

4. Two hundred (200) texts in various bindings. Was information conveyed in this manner? Many such sheets were found in ball form, stacked around the remains. Did they act as insulation? Burial practices? Further research is required.

THE GREAT EMU WAR, ENDING AND AFTERMATH: The victorious emus roamed freely on the farms, claiming their spoils and ruining the wheat fields once more. With support from the Australian Premier, farmers once again pleaded with the government to resume involvement. Meredith returned to his post and led the charge. After a rocky few days, the troops began to report killings of around one hundred emus a week. On December 10th, 1932, Meredith and his merry men were recalled by the government after firing nearly 10,000 rounds and killing around 980 birds. The Great Emu War was over.

RAPTOR:

1. A carnivorous bird with a curved beak and large sharp talons. It feeds on hunted or carrion meat.

2. A small-to-medium-sized predatory dinosaur.

AMBER

I found a bleeding

tree in my grandparents' yard.

The sap collected just below the wound,

and was curiously forming the shape

of a mouse. I was certain

this mouse would bring me fame.

I poked it.

It was hard, so I decided to pluck it

off the tree, thinking it was ripe,
but found a sticky interior.

No matter, I was a patient child, and was willing

to wait. I pocketed the mouse.

It was not until my mother—

rubbing the melted mouse

out of my freshly laundered pants—

explained to me that amber

takes millions of years to form

that I decided to find my fortune elsewhere.

A PSA from the American Dental Association: Brush Your Teeth

SCENE: Night. Anthropomorphic dinosaurs and other prehistoric animals sit around a campfire. Bright guitar music begins to play.

GRANDPA: Kids, how do we take care of our teeth?

KIDS/GRANDPA (singing): Brush your teeth twice a day, floss your teeth once a day! If you want healthy teeth, do this every day. Brush your teeth...

GRANDPA: Fight tooth decay!

KIDS: Floss your teeth...

Scene cuts to the interior of a DINOSAUR DENTIST's cave.

DENTIST: Don't forget regular dental check-ups, okay?

Cuts back to the campfire scene. Zoom out as "American Dental Association / www.ada.org" flashes on screen.

ALL: Brush your teeth twice a day, floss your teeth once a day!

Fade to black.

When I was three, my parents fed into my dinosaur obsession by giving me an illustrated encyclopedia. I learned the names and characteristics from cover to cover. When we traveled to San Diego on a family trip, I was told that we would be visiting a dinosaur park. At last, I was presented with a chance to proudly show off my vast knowledge of the prehistoric world! Since that moment, I have not felt such deep intellectual joy, and I fear it will forever lie in the recesses of my memory unparalleled... so profound was this feeling. At the hotel, I prowled slowly towards our room, investigating my surroundings, my back hunched, my hands defensively raised, my nose held up to the air. Upon reaching our door, I was ready to voice my findings with confidence: "It smells like dinosaurs!" Only a three-year-old knows what dinosaurs smell like.

Some pterosaurs (from Greek words "ptero" and "saur," meaning "wing lizard") had fur.

SOFT TISSUE FOSSILS:
Soft fossils, which are the remains of components that would usually decompose like skin or hair, are incredibly rare and usually found in areas where the organism was frozen and preserved in ice or other anaerobic conditions. Scientists can determine the approximate appearance of the organism by comparing these remains to the features of their modern-day descendants.

The existence of dinosaurs was proven in 1841. Before then, fossils were believed to be the remains of an extinct species of giants.

ICHNOFOSSILS:
Ichnofossils, also known as trace fossils, are the remnants of prehistoric activity, and are integral in the process of determining biological and behavioral characteristics. These fossils include footprints, burrows, and fossilized droppings, known as coprolites. As patterns and traits are similar amongst many species, however, it is often impossible to determine which creature produced a certain trace. To remedy this issue, such fossils are categorized by activities, as opposed to species.

Gastroliths, also known as stomach stones or gizzard stones, are used by species with insufficient grinding teeth to assist in food digestion.

The only existing fossilized Seismosaurus, a massive sauropod, is believed to have died from asphyxiation; it choked on a rock intended to be a gastrolith.

ll it takes is a big rock... Right now, Earth is unprepared to prevent an asteroid impact, which could cause tsunamis, firestorms, and impact winters, threatening mass extinction of the same scale as the episode that destroyed the dinosaurs. While the possibility of such an impact is incredibly low in the short term, it has been determined by NASA and other organizations that such an event will eventually occur.

One such rock, measuring nearly 2,000 feet across, was discovered by NASA in March 2020. Although highly unlikely, there is a chance it will hit our little blue planet on either September 10, 2074, or September 9, 2081. May the calendars be marked.

To deal with this threat, space organizations have been developing various methods of containment, one being fragmentation. The idea is to send rocket missiles or the equivalent into space to break the asteroid into pieces that will burn up when in contact with the planet's atmosphere or at least create minimal impact. Somehow, though, shooting at a big, fast-moving rock doesn't sound like the most secure idea.

Sinclair's mascot, proudly displayed on their old gasoline signs, is Dino, an Apatosaurus.

The massive Apatosaurus was discovered by paleontologist Othniel C. Marsh in 1877. When he found an even larger specimen, he named the finding Brontosaurus. Scientists later determined that it was the same species and renamed it to Apatosaurus. When the USPS issued a stamp of the creature in 1989, labeling it "Brontosaurus," many angry academics and aficionados rose up in protest, disdainfully accusing the postal service of preferring "cartoon nomenclature to scientific nomenclature." As it later turned out, the structure of the Brontosaurus bone structure is sufficiently different from that of the Apatosaurus to be named its own species, so the paleontology community revisited the name once more.

I n 2005, my family and I visited the Lowell Observatory in Flagstaff, Arizona, where Pluto was first observed in 1930. They were celebrating the 75th anniversary of that discovery and selling commemorative pins. I was raised on the following way of remembering the planets: "My Very Eager Mother Just Served Us Nine Pizzas," and proudly boasted that I knew we were in the presence of the "pizza." Pluto was a planet. There was no doubt about it. When the International Astronomical Union met to define "planet" the following year, however, they decided to play dietician and pizza was taken off the menu. I was devastated. Heartbroken. What would be the next pneumonic device? I began to feel the nihilism that sweeps over every five-year-old in such a moment, for Pluto was my favorite planet. Whatever happened to supporting the underdog? Nothing made sense! Pluto is dead, and we killed him!

In that 2006 IAU conference, Pluto was reclassified as a "dwarf planet," which is essentially a consolation prize for large asteroids and other space rocks. I wonder if Pluto will one day set its sights on our presumptuous little planet and take its revenge.

One of my favorite film franchises growing up was *The Land Before Time.* David Hepworth, from *Empire,* described it as such: "Sharp animation and powerful visualization of scale will enthrall a young audience but the clumsy cub-scout moralizing feels, well, extinct."

IMPRINTS: Imprints are the molds of thin organisms, like ferns and trilobites. They are often found in sandstone and ash.

When I was around four or five, my grandmother taught me the ancient practice of pressing leaves and flowers. My favorite flowers were ones she called "Lion's Yawn." The violet flower could be opened to reveal a yellow interior and small, pollen-covered stigmas, resembling a tongue inside the flower's maw. My grandmother would pry them open and roar, stretching her smiling wrinkles, and I would laugh. I pressed those flowers in my books, probably the dinosaur encyclopedia since the covers were heavy, but I won't lie and pretend to remember. If I ever find them, I wonder if their exposure to fresh air will make them yawn.

Dinosaur Scales and Other Vocal Warmups for Singers (Patent Pending)

1. Pterodactyl's Yawn: Force a yawn, and as you exhale, emit a horrifying screech that will tingle the spines of your enemies.

2. Argentinosaurus Arpeggios: Engage in the following bouncy, major scale arpeggio: Do, Mi, Sol, Do, Sol, Mi, Do, while making a "caw" sound.

3. T-Rex Jaw Drops: Open your mouth, place your pointer fingers in the cavities that form on the end of your mandible (near the ear), and sing the previously mentioned arpeggio, making sure that your jaw is dropping enough to form that little space.

4. Brachiosaurus Bellows: For this exercise, choose a note in your falsetto range and sing it on a "Hoo." Then, slide down an octave from that note, changing to an "Ah" sound. Make your way up and down the scale, reaching your highest and lowest notes.

Another PSA from the ADA: Baby Teeth with Dudley the Dinosaur

SCENE: Inside the Dinosaur home. The family is looking into a baby pen, where DEEDEE plays.

DUDLEY: Grandpa, Baby Deedee got his first tooth!

A montage featuring scenes emblematic of GRANDPA's speech ensues.

GRANDPA: Sure has! Strong baby teeth are important. They help Baby chew his food easily, learn to speak correctly, smile and look attractive. We should schedule a dental visit by his first birthday.

DUDLEY: Good oral health is important...

GRANDPA: Even for an old dinosaur like me. Brush twice a day, floss once a day, limit between-meal snacks, get regular check-ups so that smile can stay healthy for a lifetime.

Close-up on DEEDEE in the pen as "American Dental Association and your Local Dental Society www.ada. org" flashes on screen before...

Blackout.

This poster has been on my bedroom door since December 4th, 2004. At first, I was disappointed when I found out that these dinosaurs were not drawn to scale and that I was not, in fact, nearing the height of a velociraptor. I soon got over it, and since then, the creatures have faithfully held onto this information. They are frozen now, a fossil record buried and obsolete since my height flatlined during my sophomore year of high school. Perhaps this will come in handy again when I am in my thirties and begin to shrink...

At the University of Connecticut's Storrs campus, there is a rock resting beside Beach Hall. There are no guardrails around it, no markings of any kind, so I spent a semester passing this humble relic on my way to classes, my eyes sparing no more than a quick, glazed glance as I would go over a summary of *The Little Clay Cart* or the symbolism in an Elizabeth Bishop poem. It was not until I enrolled in a geology course during my second semester that I began to make the distinction between a gneiss rock and a schist one, noting the various formations of the landscape that surrounded me.

It was on yet another everyday pilgrimage to class that my recently geologically enlightened eyes discovered the Adidas-symbol-looking protrusions on the stone: a sign of three that inspired my curiosity. In my mind, there is a plaque with the epitaph, "Here lies a fossil, a footprint of an unknown being I will never meet or see or smell or hear." The self-preserving side of me rejoices in this fact, as it elicits a memory of walking home from school to find a mother bear in my path; now, if only that bear were ten times larger, a biped, and roared (or peeped, we will never know).

The analytical side, however, the one that hungers for answers and growls against the self-preserving side that desperately tries to arrange a ceasefire ("I'm begging you, no more Wikipedia, you have an eight a.m. tomorrow, the dinosaurs aren't going anywhere, they've been dead for millions of years, they'll be there tomorrow"), laments the impossibility of such an encounter. The only compromise I can arrange with myself is the meditation on a footprint.

O n Tuesday, August 15, 2019, students of Bristol Eastern High School (my alma mater) found what may be Eubrontes tracks: a footprint resembling the three-toed print located at the University of Connecticut. This specimen was discovered during the creation of a rain garden on the school's territory. It now lies on display in one of the school's glass cases.

Eubrontes, Connecticut's state fossil, is a common find in the Connecticut River Valley, and thousands of examples can be found at Dinosaur State Park in Rocky Hill. There is speculation that the rock found at BEHS is not local, however, but was taken from elsewhere in the state and deposited during the process of converting the swamp land on which the school now stands into solid ground.

There is a genre of erotic fiction that involves humans in conversation with dinosaurs. Notable titles include Taken by the T-Rex, Ravished by Triceratops, *and* A Billionaire Dinosaur Forced Me Gay. *Theorists posit that this genre stems from the appeal of the impossible. The unattainable nature of the situation frees the imagination to fantasize about more risky behaviors than one would normally engage with. There is still a debate over whether these pieces are written ironically, and it is highly unlikely that we will ever know the truth.*

The front legs of a T-Rex were not much longer than human arms.

YET ANOTHER PSA FROM THE ADA: BRUSH AND FLOSS!

SCENE: Inside GRANDPA's fishing cabin. Twilight.

GRANDPA: Before we go fishing, Dudley, let's brush.

DUDLEY (surprised): Grandpa, you still brush your teeth?

GRANDPA: Every day of my life!

Wipe transition to the bathroom. DUDLEY is brushing his teeth.

GRANDPA: Regular check-ups, brush twice a day to stop tooth decay, floss once a day.

DUDLEY (even more surprised): You floss?

GRANDPA: Well, sure, to stop the plaque that causes gum disease: a leading cause of tooth loss in adult dinosaurs like me.

Fade to a lake behind the cabin. DUDLEY and GRANDPA are fishing. A toothless old dinosaur reels in a large fish.

TOOTHLESS DINOSAUR: Oh, I got one!

Triumphant trumpet music plays as the camera zooms in on a close-up of TOOTHLESS DINOSAUR's face.
ENSEMBLE: Brush and floss!

Blackout.

What I don't understand is why they chose dinosaurs, or why the dinosaurs have to brush their teeth before they go fishing. Is it just for the age jokes with Grandpa? That's such a low pay-off. They could have chosen any beings. Besides, how would a T-Rex (which is what I believe their species to be, though I may be mistaken because of the artistic liberties) even reach its mouth to brush with those short arms? The ADA really sacrificed relatability and credibility with these choices. Nevertheless, the "Dudley Dinosaur" public service announcements have been etched into the gray matter of my mind. No fall or blow to the head could expel these songs and scripts from my memory. "Brush your teeth twice a day, floss your teeth once a day! If you want healthy teeth, do this every day" gets stuck in my head probably once a month.

Avimimus
/ah-vi-MEEM-us/
noun

My favorite dinosaur, meaning "bird mimic." A small, omnivorous theropod (feathered biped) from the Late Cretaceous Period.

Rock Star

I've passed Pluto and Saturn
And all forms of matter,
But it all seems quite pointless to me.
Don't belong in the Kuiper,
I am an outsider
And I don't know where I'm meant to be.

The planets and stars have it easy:
Each has its ellipsis to chart.
Meanwhile, I'm going without any knowing
Where I am to make a new start.

I'm a rock star
With no audience
Of no consequence.
I can't make an impact alone!
I'm a rock star,
Hurtling through space
At a dizzying pace,
Looking for a place to call "home,"
Looking for a place to call "home."

There's a planet before me
I hope won't ignore me,
It seems lonely with only one moon.
I hope it's accepting.
I'm nearing and melting

And I'll finally find my place soon!

I know that warm water will welcome
Me as friend, and not asteroid.
Name-calling is finished, I won't be diminished
With nicknames like "space hemorrhoid."

I'm a rock star
With no audience,
Of no consequence.
I can't make an impact alone!
I'm a rock star,
Hurtling through space
At a dizzying pace,
Looking for a place to call "home,"
Looking for a place to call "home."

I know there I can make a difference.

At last, I will make history!

On that small, green-blue planet,

On that small, green-blue planet,

On that small, green-blue planet,

I'll be a rock star, wait and see.

www.ingramcontent.com/pod-product-compliance
Lightning Source LLC
Chambersburg PA
CBHW022106020426
42335CB00012B/857